Client Confidentiality and Privileged Communications

NASW PRESS

National Association of Social Workers
Washington, DC

Jeanne W. Anastas, *PhD, LMSW, President*
Elizabeth J. Clark, *PhD, ACSW, MPH, Executive Director*

Introduction

A majority of the legal concerns raised by individual National Association of Social Workers [NASW] members involve questions relating to the privacy of clients' mental health treatment information. For many people, the acronym "HIPAA" (Health Insurance Portability and Accountability Act) has become synonymous with health care privacy; however, the underlying principles of confidentiality and privilege remain fundamental to any analysis of patient privacy. Applying the concepts of confidentiality and privilege to the professional services provided by social workers requires an understanding of federal health privacy laws and regulations, as well as state law standards and ethical obligations. This *Law Note* discusses the applicable principles and outlines some of the exceptions to them, particularly in the context of clinical social work practice.

In an era of rapid change in information technology capacity, society is experiencing a paradigm shift that impacts expectations about privacy; however, the fundamental need for confidentiality remains as a lynchpin to successful mental health treatment and effective social worker interventions.

> Mental health professionals have long recognized the importance of confidentiality to successful diagnosis and treatment of human suffering. Clients are only willing to reveal their innermost thoughts and feelings when they are secure in the belief that their therapist will never reveal the information to others inappropriately. Therefore, disclosure without the client's consent, although permissible in some circumstances, threatens one of the fundamental precepts that enables psychotherapy to work.[5]

The duty of the social worker to keep the confidences of a client is reinforced by the fact that a *Code* violation can be based on the social worker's failure to do so.[6] In addition, inappropriate disclosure of a client's confidences can be grounds for a malpractice suit for breach of confidentiality,[7] a breach of contract suit,[8] or for a licensure board complaint.[9]

When a specific situation does arise requiring the possible or necessary revelation of a client's records or communications, clear guidance is frequently not available. Moreover, many social workers are not trained in the intricacies of law or ethics and find themselves conflicted about loyalty to their clients, concerns about meeting ethical and legal responsibilities, and worries about their own potential liability. Applying the concepts of confidentiality and privilege requires a basic understanding of the meaning of the terms and the trend of legal developments around each term.

Scope of Confidentiality

The Social Work Dictionary defines confidentiality as:

> A principle of ethics according to which the social worker or other professional may not disclose information about a client without the client's consent. This information includes the identity of the client, content of verbalizations, professional opinions about the client, and material from records. Confidentiality does not preclude the communications of pertinent information about the client to relevant colleagues, in the worker's agency. In specific circumstances, social workers and other professionals may be compelled by law to reveal to designated authorities some information (such as threats of violence, commission of crimes, and suspected child abuse) that would be relevant to legal judgments.[10]

Confidential communications must occur in a setting where privacy is reasonably expected. This would generally be in the course of consultation, diagnosis, therapy or treatment and would also include eligibility determinations, referral information, and chart reviews. The legal protections for confidentiality found in a variety of legal sources can be complicated by the layers of analysis that may be necessary to identify the degree and type of protection to be accorded client records in a particular setting.

Some state statutes specifically define the scope of confidentiality for social work records.[11] These statutes may be incorporated in licensing acts, licensing board regulations for social workers, or evidence laws applying the rules of privilege. In many states, medical records statutes define what an inpatient medical record is, what it should contain, and to whom it may be made available with or without the consent of the patient or client.[12] Outpatient, primary care, and private practice therapy records may be less well defined, and access to social work records may or may not be clearly delineated.

The HIPAA medical privacy regulations define "protected health information" (PHI) to include all individually identifiable health information that a health care provider (or health plan) "creates, maintains, receives or transmits" about the patient.[13] Patient access to their PHI is a mandatory right within the HIPAA regulations, although this does not extend to "psychotherapy notes" if they are maintained separately from the medical record.[14]

From a professional ethics standpoint, all documentation and information related to or obtained from a client or patient should be viewed as confidential, whether or not a specific law or regulation defines it as a confidential medical record.

Obtaining Client Consent

In an ethical sense, a breach of confidentiality involves the release of confidential client-related information without the client's informed written or oral consent. In a legal sense, a breach of confidentiality involves the violation of a statutory, regulatory, or common law requirement to maintain the confidentiality of a client's information and records. There is no breach of confidentiality if the client, who is competent to do so, has consented to the release of information within the specific circumstances.[15] An appropriate release may be executed at the commencement of treatment to permit records or reports to be sent to an insurance company, referring physicians, or other likely third party requesters who have a professional need to know the information. The client should be made aware of the scope and intent of the release.

Within the specific limitations of state law, consent to release information can be obtained from

- a legally competent adult;
- the legal guardian of an adult found to be legally incompetent;
- an emancipated minor as defined under state law;

were now faced with legal liability for their failure to warn. Section 43.92 was intended to

> limit the psychotherapists' liability for failure to warn ... [in] those circumstances where the patient has communicated an actual threat of violence against an identified victim, and to abolish the expansive rulings of *Tarasoff* ... that a therapist can be held liable for the mere failure to predict and warn of potential violence by his patient.[44]

This statute allows disclosure of confidential communications "if the psychotherapist has reasonable cause to believe that, as a result of a mental or emotional condition, the patient is dangerous to the person or property of himself or another, and that only through disclosure can the threatened danger be prevented."[45] A "psychotherapist," as defined for the purpose of this statute, includes social workers and other mental health care providers.[46]

The *Tarasoff* and *Thompson* decisions brought into focus a difficult public policy dilemma. Once a state recognizes the duty of a therapist to breach a patient's confidentiality to protect third parties from a potentially dangerous client, what is the extent of that duty? Is the duty triggered only when there is a clearly identified and specifically threatened victim, or does that duty extend to the general public and more amorphous threats? Reflecting this policy debate, state laws today fall into roughly three groups. Some states recognize a duty to warn when there is a general threat or a threat against the public at large.[47] Others states recognize the duty only against a specific threat to a readily identifiable victim.[48] Other states have yet to address the issue or have not recognized any such duty at all or,[49] while ostensibly recognizing such a duty, have yet to encounter a situation in which they are willing to impose it.[50] The remaining states do not fall into any one group. Iowa for example does allow social workers to disclose confidential information when "the information reveals the contemplation or commission of a crime."[51] However, the law does not specify whether the crime also needs to constitute a threat to a specific person or even a general threat to the public. Other states allow disclosure in judicial proceeding, but are silent on whether social workers may disclose that same information without a subpoena.[52]

States following the first approach are willing to sacrifice confidentiality at a low threshold of certainty, thus placing the greatest emphasis on protection of the public. They leave the most discretion to the mental health professional. For example, in Illinois, the social worker may disclose confidential communications to "protect any person from a clear, imminent risk of serious mental or physical harm or injury, or to forestall a serious threat to the public safety."[53] Under this formulation, there is no requirement that the identity of the victim be known. The threat can be a harm to the general public and need not be as dire as death or even involve physical injury. Although these statutes tend to be permissive, *allowing* but not *requiring* disclosure, some courts are inclined to read "may" as "must" and impose a duty to warn.[54]

Massachusetts, in the second group of states, maintains that confidentiality should be breached only in cases where there is great certainty of harm. The duty exists only when the client communicates "an explicit threat to kill or inflict serious bodily injury upon a reasonably identified victim or victims and the client has the apparent intent and ability to carry out the threat or has a history of physical violence which is known to the social worker ... "[55] There is great particularity required in this formulation: specificity in knowing the identity of the victim, the severity of the harm threatened, and the likelihood that the patient will carry out the threat.

In the third group of states, the law does not impose a duty on any mental health professionals to warn of a patient's dangerous inclinations, either because the courts have rejected such a duty as unreasonable,[56] or because they have not had occasion to address the issue.[57]

Past Criminal Acts

Unlike the duty to alert potential victims to the threat a client poses, states generally do not require social workers to report prior criminal acts or harmful acts of the client unless the victim is a child or, in most states, an elderly or vulnerable adult. However, some states permit but do not require the disclosure of client confidences that reveal past commission of other crimes.[58] Even though some states may permit disclosure of prior criminal acts, many factors should enter into a social worker's decision about whether to take such a step. The ethical rule should be observed that a "compelling professional reason" would provide the prime motivation, and all facts and ethical or legal principles supporting the decision should be documented. Whether a social worker may be compelled to testify about a client's past criminal acts in a legal proceeding is reviewed below in the section on privilege.

Child Abuse or Neglect

All states require that a mental health professional report known or suspected cases of child abuse or neglect.[59] The now universal requirement that child abuse and neglect be reported to appropriate authorities reflects the national concern about this problem as well as the federal role in funding programs to stem child abuse.[60] Indeed, the majority of cases dealing with disclosure of confidential or privileged communications without client consent are cases involving children.[61] These laws reflect the policy that protection of children supersedes the preservation of the privacy of individuals. Reporting of child abuse and neglect is generally protected by immunity from suit under state law.[62]

serious injury, when disclosure is necessary to investigate or prosecute a serious crime, or when the client has raised an issue related to his or her treatment in legal proceedings. The Substance Abuse and Mental Health Services Administration ("SAMHSA") has published an educational document, *Frequently Asked Questions: Applying the Substance Abuse Confidentiality Regulations to Health Information Exchange.*[78] These answers do not provide new regulations, but are an agency interpretation of the existing confidentiality regulations for the disclosure of drug abuse and alcoholism treatment records and information.

Clients' health records in many instances are now being maintained and transmitted in electronic format. One model for handling health data involves third parties, who serve as the electronic repositories of protected health information. These technological advances and organizational models have raised issues regarding the confidentiality standards that govern the third party repository's access to a patient's protected information and access by other parties, such as health insurers and other health care providers. SAMHSA's answers explain how federal confidentiality regulations apply to the electronic exchange of drug and alcohol abuse treatment information in "Health Information Exchanges." A review of the SAMHSA document is highly recommended for social workers who provide services to clients in drug and alcohol treatment programs (see Appendix B).

Although SAMHSA's *FAQs* interpret the same regulatory standard for the release of drug and alcohol abuse treatment information that has been in existence for several decades, by allowing a third party (the HIO) to act as an electronic "gatekeeper," the determination of what constitutes an emergency warranting a nonconsensual violation of the client's privacy is shifted from the drug and alcohol abuse treatment provider (the "Part 2" provider) to the emergency care provider. The difference in perspective of these two providers creates a potentially significant change in the client's level of privacy. Emergency care providers are more likely to perceive a need to access the client's information, whereas the Part 2 providers, who may be social workers, are apt to be more protective of the client's privacy and to more narrowly interpret the need for sensitive information to be disclosed. This issue has not been formally studied; however, it is likely that the transition to electronic health records may result in an increase in disclosures for emergency treatment purposes.

Privilege and the Release of Client Information in Legal Proceedings

Privileged communication is an important subcategory or characteristic of confidential communications.[79] The "privilege" is the client's legal right to keep certain communications with the social worker private and not available as evidence in legal proceedings, including subpoenas of records, pretrial depositions or affidavits, and testimony at trial. It parallels other evidentiary privileges, such as the common law spousal privilege[80] and the constitutionally guaranteed privilege against self-incrimination.[81] Privilege serves to prevent the social worker from being a witness against a client's wishes or best therapeutic interests.

The privilege against disclosure of confidential communications in legal proceedings is a matter of public policy. It is grounded in the community value that the patient should be confident that his or her innermost thoughts can be revealed in confidence without being subject to public exposure.[82] It is intended to protect the client from humiliation, embarrassment, or disgrace and to promote mental health treatment. As such, it is a right of the client, not the social worker. Although the social worker is obligated to assert the client's privilege when records or testimony are demanded, if the client waives the privilege, the social worker must accede.[83]

By definition, privilege keeps information out of the knowledge of those who are called on to resolve disputes and vindicate rights. There is a conflict between privacy rights of the client and the need to promote use of therapy, on the one hand, and the search for truth and justice, on the other hand. Similar to the discussion about breach of confidentiality, as a society we are forced to balance two sets of competing values and to establish ground rules by which to be guided. The result is a few exceptional situations in which courts or legislatures have determined that privilege should not apply or that a client, by bringing a certain type of legal action, has waived his or her right to privilege.

The most widely accepted group of exceptions is once again in the area of protection of children. Most states make exceptions to privilege in matters of child custody, adoption, and termination of parental rights.[84] However, where a social worker has an obligation to report occurrences of child abuse learned from a client to protect the child, courts will not necessarily allow that same information in the criminal proceeding against the perpetrator.[85] In weighing the importance of admitting confidential communications, courts will consider whether there are other sources for similar evidence, making the confidential communications duplicative. In spite of the protections of privilege, clients may be presumed to have effectively waived the protection by filing certain types of lawsuits or taking certain actions. Some of these waivers are generally accepted, while others may vary from state to state.

A written waiver or release signed by a competent person in the context of a legal proceeding is generally accepted as an effective waiver of privilege. Independent disclosure by a client to a third party may or may not constitute a waiver, depending on the circumstances and state law. Many states consider that the client has waived the privilege when his or her mental health is made an issue in either a civil or criminal case. For example, in a civil case, if a patient is suing a third party for pain and suffering or emotional distress or suing a social worker for malpractice, the client's records will not be held to be privileged because the content of the records is central to the claim being adjudicated.[86] In a criminal case, where a client is pleading a defense of insanity or diminished capacity, access to mental health records will also be granted. Disclosure will be limited, however, to the client's mental or emotional condition and may not be used as evidence of whether he or she committed the crime.[87]

Although it is possible to make the distinction between confidentiality and privilege, many state statutes use the two terms interchangeably, and one must sometimes glean from the context whether the law was intended to create a privilege or mandate confidentiality. Because privilege arises when determining whether evidence is admissible in a judicial proceeding, privilege rules are most logically found within a state's evidence code. However, with the increasing recognition of the social work profession as a significant provider of mental health treatment and evaluation, many legislatures have grafted privilege rules onto social work professional licensing codes. When the privilege appears in the professional code, rather than the evidence code, it may not be clear whether exceptions to privilege that have been carved out for other professions (e.g., psychologists or physicians) within the evidence code are equally applicable to the social work profession.

Federal Treatment of Privilege

The federal law of evidence was clarified by the U.S. Supreme Court's decision in *Jaffee v. Redmond*,[88] to confirm that client communications with licensed social workers in the context of psychotherapy are privileged communications under the federal rules of evidence. Therefore, these communications are generally not subject to disclosure as evidence in the federal courts. The U.S. Supreme Court's majority opinion accorded much weight to the fact that the "psychotherapist privilege is rooted in the imperative need for confidence and trust."[89] The U.S.

Supreme Court contrasted the physician's need for medical facts with the psychotherapists' dependence on

> an atmosphere of confidence and trust in which the patient is willing to make a frank and complete disclosure of facts, emotions memories and fears. Because of the sensitive nature of the problems for which individuals consult psychotherapists, disclosure of confidential communications made during counseling sessions may cause embarrassment or disgrace. For this reason, the mere possibility of disclosure may impede development of the confidential relationship necessary for successful treatment.[90]

This need for frank and open discussion and revelation of innermost thoughts in psychotherapy requires protection from public disclosure. The U.S. Supreme Court in *Jaffee* concluded that both private and public interests would be served by treating communications between the psychotherapist and client as privileged. The public interest to be protected was defined by the U.S. Supreme Court as "the provision of appropriate treatment for individuals suffering the effects of a mental or emotional problem."[91] With a vote of confidence to the value of psychotherapy, the U.S. Supreme Court concluded that

> [the] mental health of our citizenry, no less than its physical health, is a public good of transcendent importance.
>
> In contrast to the significant public and private interests supporting recognition of the privilege, the likely evidentiary benefit that would result from the denial of the privilege is modest. If the privilege were rejected, confidential conversations between psychotherapists and their patients would surely be chilled, particularly when it is obvious that the circumstances that give rise to the need for treatment will probably result in litigation. Without a privilege, much of the desirable evidence to which litigants such as petitioner seek access—for example, admissions against interest by a party—is likely to come into being. This unspoken "evidence" will therefore serve no great truth-seeking function than if it had been spoken and privileged.
>
> That it is appropriate for the federal courts to recognize a psychotherapist privilege under Rule 501 is confirmed by the fact that all 50 States and the District of Columbia have enacted into law some form of psychotherapist privilege. We have previously observed that the policy decisions of the State bear on the question whether federal courts should recognize a new privilege or amend the coverage of an existing one.[92]

The U.S. Supreme Court viewed the evidentiary benefit to be gained by revelation of communications during psychotherapy as limited and the negative or chilling effect on treatment as great.

In its opinion in *Jaffee,* the U.S. Supreme Court's majority also concluded "without hesitation" that the federal psychotherapy privilege should extend to clients of licensed social workers.[93] NASW had submitted an amicus curiae (friend of the court) brief in support of that position. The U.S. Supreme Court relied on that brief to reach its conclusion.[94] The U.S. Supreme Court reasoned:

> Today, social workers provide a significant amount of mental health treatment. See, *e.g.,* ... Brief for National Association of Social Workers et al. as *Amici Curiae* 5–7 ... Their clients often include the poor and those of modest means who could not afford the assistance of a psychiatrist or psychologist, *id.,* at 6–7 (citing authorities), but whose counseling sessions serve the same public goals. Perhaps in recognition of these circumstances, the vast majority of States explicitly extend a testimonial privilege to licensed social workers.[95]

In the years since *Jaffee* was decided, federal courts have used its reasoning to further clarify the psychotherapist privilege. For example in 2004, the U.S. Court of Appeals for the Eighth Circuit addressed whether a criminal defendant had a right to access the psychiatric records of a government witness for purposes of cross-examination.[96] The Eighth Circuit upheld the lower court's denial to the defendant's discovery request. They found that under *Jaffee* "the district court did not abuse its discretion in denying Mr. Newton's [defendant] request that it authorize discovery or conduct an *in camera* [in chambers] review of the psychiatric records."[97]

"Dangerous Patient Exception"

In footnote 19 of the *Jaffee* majority opinion, the U.S. Supreme Court left the door open for possible exceptions to the psychotherapist–patient privilege. The footnote states:

> Although it would be premature to speculate about most future developments in the federal psychotherapist privilege, we do not doubt that there are situations in which the privilege must give way, for example, if a serious threat of harm to the patient or to others can be averted only by means of a disclosure by the therapist.[98]

Since *Jaffee,* federal courts have been faced with the task of interpreting the language of footnote 19 and any exceptions that it may have created. In *U.S. v. Glass,*[99] the U.S. Court of Appeals for the Tenth Circuit "applied a 'dangerous patient' exception, drawing on *Jaffee*'s footnote 19."[100] In that case, Mr. Glass moved to exclude from his criminal trial a confidential statement made to his psychotherapist relaying his desire to kill President Clinton. The government argued the threat to the president created a "duty to protect," which allowed the psychotherapist to disclose Glass's statement, and subsequently made the statement admissible during Glass's trial.[101] The court agreed that a "dangerous patient" exception to the psychotherapist–patient privilege did exist under *Jaffee*. However the court found under the facts of this case, the exception was inapplicable and excluded the statement from Glass's trial.

Other federal courts have disagreed with the Tenth Circuit, and found no such exception was created by footnote 19. In *U.S. v. Hayes,* the U.S. Court of Appeals for the Sixth Circuit held there was no "dangerous patient" exception to the psychotherapist–patient privilege in criminal proceedings.[102] In *Hayes,* the defendant communicated his desire to harm his supervisor during psychotherapy sessions. While the court recognized the therapist's statutory duty to warn the intended victim, it did not recognize a separate "dangerous patient" exception that would allow the defendant's psychotherapy records or his therapist's testimony to be admissible in criminal proceedings.[103] Similarly in 2003, the U.S. Court of Appeals for the Ninth Circuit also refused to recognize a "dangerous patient" exception in criminal proceedings.[104]

The circuits are clearly split on the existence of a "dangerous patient" exception. To further confuse the issue, the Fifth Circuit has cited *Jaffee*'s requirement that privilege only cover *confidential communications* to decide the matter.[105] In *U.S. v. Auster,* the court allowed threats the defendant made against his workers compensation claim managers during therapy sessions to be admitted in his criminal trial. The court reasoned that once the defendant was made aware of his therapist's statutory duty to report such threats, he had no expectation of confidentiality in any future threats communicated during therapy.[106] Therefore the U.S. Supreme Court found privilege did not apply, and the statements were admissible evidence. *Auster* was appealed to the U.S. Supreme Court, a perfect opportunity for the court to resolve the confusion over *Jaffee*'s meaning, however the court declined to hear the case.[107]

"In all of the above cases the courts were applying the principles articulated in *Jaffee,* a civil lawsuit, to criminal prosecutions where normally different rules of legal procedure apply. Thus, it remains unanswered by the federal appellate courts how a "dangerous patient" case would be interpreted in a civil litigation."[108]

State Treatment of Privilege

Although the *Jaffee* ruling is not automatically applicable to cases brought in state courts, the holding could have great influence on state court decision making in several ways.[109] First, a state court would find ample support to confirm a state law's grant of privilege in fact situations that might have otherwise been questionable. For example, in *In Re Berg,*[110] a parent during a custody dispute wanted access to his children's therapy records. The children's therapists refused. The Supreme Court of New Hampshire held the records to be privileged, even though the children's own parent wanted to waive the privilege. The New Hampshire Supreme Court cited *Jaffee v. Redmond* in support of its decision, to explain the importance and sanctity of the therapist–client privilege.[111]

In 20 states and the District of Columbia, statutes grant privilege to communications between clients and mental health professionals.[112] These "generic" privilege laws generally consider communications with psychiatrists, psychologists, social workers, and other listed mental health professionals as having equivalent importance and rights to privacy. In 26 states, privilege is granted to social workers as a profession, and separate statutes identify the privilege granted to other mental health professions.[113] In two states, courts or legislatures have explicitly denied any privilege to communications with social workers.[114] In two states, it is unclear whether all such communications are privileged, because there is no general statutory provision or the courts have had no opportunity to adjudicate the issue.[115]

The "generic" privilege laws applicable to the mental health professions in a state offer the best protection to the client, who may not be familiar with the varying educational and licensing requirements among the many mental health professions. Moreover, a generic privilege focuses on the services provided because privilege is accorded to client communications with all licensed mental health professionals who provide similar services.

The social worker–client specific privilege statutes provide considerable protection to the client but have one shortcoming. If they are worded differently than the psychotherapist or other privilege statutes, courts may assume that the legislature intended the social worker privilege to be different in scope than that of the other mental health professions and may give unequal treatment to similar fact situations involving differently licensed mental health professionals. To avoid this problem, legislatures should include social workers in the definition of psychotherapist for the purpose of privilege,[116] provide that the privilege granted to social workers will be the same as that for psychotherapists,[117] or grant the privilege in terms of the right of the client to confidential mental health treatment and reference the professional titles of all appropriate licensed providers.[118]

In the two states where there is no social worker privilege established, courts or legislatures have declared that communications with social workers do not warrant the same protection as communications with psychiatrists or psychologists.[119] In view of the prevalence of social workers as the major providers of mental health care treatment in the United States and the Supreme Court's ruling in *Jaffee,* this minority view is a disservice to the clients who are the recipients of social work in those states and is contrary to the professional and legal standards accepted in majority of the states.

Conclusion

Confidentiality of client communications is one of the ethical foundations of the social work profession and has been made a legal obligation in most states. The HIPAA Privacy Rule has heightened the general awareness of privacy rights; however, its application in relation to state social worker confidentiality laws creates an additional layer of complexity for practitioners to navigate when a specific situation arises. The social work profession must work toward increasing the universality and uniformity of state laws protecting client confidentiality and privilege. The different uses of the terms and lack of common agreement on meanings creates confusion in applying general rules to specific situations. By being aware of the requirements of the state in which the social worker practices and working for consistent treatment of licensed mental health professionals based on the nature of the services provided, the social worker will be better able to serve the needs of the client and to further the advancement of the social work profession.

Endnotes

1. National Association of Social Workers [hereafter, NASW], *Code of Ethics* (2008), *available at* http://www.naswdc.org/pubs/code/code.asp.

2. NASW, *Confidentiality and Information Utilization,* SOCIAL WORK SPEAKS (8th ed. 2009).

3. *See* NASW, *Code of Ethics* (1994)

   "Social Worker's Ethical Responsibility to Clients"

   1. The social worker should share with others confidences revealed by clients, without their consent, only for compelling professional reasons.
   2. The social worker should inform clients fully about the limits of confidentiality in a given situation, the purposes for which information is obtained, and how it may be used.
   3. The social worker should afford clients reasonable access to any official social work records concerning them.
   4. When providing clients with access to records, the social worker should take due care to protect the confidences of others contained in those records.
   5. The social worker should obtain informed consent of clients before taping, recording, or permitting third party observation of their activities.

   see also, NASW, *NASW Standards for Clinical Social Work in Social Work Practice* (2005), *available at* http://www.socialworkers.org/practice/standards/NASWClinicalSWStandards.pdf.

4. *See supra* note 1, at §5.02(l).

5. Gary Ford, ETHICAL REASONING FOR MENTAL HEALTH PROFESSIONALS, 93 (2006); *see also,* U.S. Department of Health and Human Services, *Confidentiality of Mental Health Information,* MENTAL HEALTH: A REPORT OF THE SURGEON GENERAL (1999), citing *Jaffee, available at* http://www.surgeongeneral.gov/library/mentalhealth/chapter7/sec1.html.

6. *See* NASW, *NASW Procedures for Professional Review Revised* (4th Ed. 2005).

7. *Doe v. Community Health Plan-Kaiser Corp.,* 709 N.Y.S.2d 215, 218 (N.Y. App. Div. 2000) ("communications to be fostered in the social worker/client relationship are confidential and a plaintiff is entitled to invoke the privilege of professional confidence a breach of which is actionable as a tort."); *see also, Dawkins v. Richmond Community Hosp.,* 30 Va. Cir. 377, Not Reported in S.E.2d, 1993 WL 946057 Va.Cir.Ct. 1993.

8. *Harley v. Druzba,* 169 A.D.2d 1001 (N.Y. App. Div. 1991); *see also, Martino v. Family Service Agency of Adams County,* 112 Ill. App. 3d 593, 600 (Ill. App. Ct. 1982).

9. *In the Matter of Michael Stevens, LCSW,* Case No. 2007–3 (Board of Clinical Social Workers of the State of Oregon 2008) (Board imposed penalty of $1,000 for Stevens unlawful disclosure of client's confidential information) *available at* http://www.oregon.gov/BLSW/pdfs/SpecificCases/LCSW_2581.pdf; *see also, Petition of Sprague,* 564 A.2d 829 (N.H.,1989).

10. Robert L. Barker, THE SOCIAL WORK DICTIONARY, 90 (5th ed., 2003); *see also,* Weiner & Wettstein, p. 203.

11. G.L. Perlman, *Mastering the Law of Privileged Communication: A Guide for Social Workers,* 33 Social Work 425 (1988); *see also,* Ala. Admin. Code r. 850-X-9-.01(2)(c)(3), 210 Ill. Comp. Stat. Ann. 85/6.17.

12. *See* Colo. State Board of Social Workers Rules, Rule 18; Mass. Regs. Code tit. 258, § 22.02; Wash. Admin. Code § 246–810–035.

13. *See* Health Insurance Portability and Accountability Act of 1996 [hereafter HIPAA], *available at* http://aspe.hhs.gov/admnsimp/pl104191.htm.

14. 45 C.F.R. § 160.103, §164.501.

15. *See* NASW, *Code of Ethics,* Section 1.07(b) ("social workers may disclose confidential information where appropriate with valid consent from a client or a person legally authorized to consent on behalf of a client").

16. Weiner & Wettstein, p. 203.

17. *See Standards for the Practice of Clinical Social Work, supra* note 3.

18. *infra*, p. 13.

19. NASW, *Code of Ethics*, Section 1.07(j).

20. *See* HIPAA, *available at* http://aspe.hhs.gov/admnsimp/pl104191.htm.

21. NASW, *The Social Worker and Protection of Privacy, available at* http://www.socialworkers.org/ldf/lawnotes/privacy.asp.

22. *Id.* (citing 45 C.F.R. § 164.508).

23. *See* NASW, *Code of Ethics*, §1.07(j).

24. NASW, *supra* note 22.

25. *See* 45 C.F.R. §164.502 ("Permitted uses and disclosures. A covered entity is permitted to use or disclose protected health information as follows: (i) to the individual; (ii) For treatment, payment, or health care operations ... ").

26. McKinney's CPLR §4508 (" ... as the client may authorize; ... the contemplation of a crime or harmful act; 3. where the client is a child under the age of sixteen and the information acquired ... indicates that the client has been the victim or subject of a crime ... where the client waives the privilege by bringing charges against such social worker and such charges involve confidential communications between the client and the social worker").

27. 45 C.F.R. §164.512.

28. *See* §164.512(b) public health purposes also includes disclosure to a public health authority authorized by law to collect health reports, disclosure to a "person subject to the jurisdiction of the Food and Drug Administration (FDA) with respect to an FDA-regulated product or activity for which the person has responsibility, ... " disclosure to a person potentially exposed to a communicable disease or at risk of contracting such a disease when authorized by law to make such a disclosure during a public health intervention or investigation, disclosure by an employer's health care provider about employees after employees have been given notice that their protected information may be disclosed to the employer.

29. Applies when required by law or when the individual agrees to disclose, *see* 164.512(c); *see also*, §§164.512(c)(2)(i)-(ii) (unless an exception applies, the individual must be promptly informed after such a disclosure).

30. §164.512(d) (includes audits, investigations, disciplinary actions, oversight of the health care system, etc.); *see also*, §164.512(d)(2) (oversight does not include investigations of the individual not related to the receipt of health care, public benefits, etc.).

31. Other examples include a discovery request after the party seeking information has given assurances that the individual (subject of the health information) has been given notice of the request or the party seeking the information has sought a protective order, *see* §164.512(e), §164.512(e)(vi) (covered entity can also be the one to provide notice to individual or seek protective order); *see also*, NASW, *Social Workers, HIPAA, and Subpoenas* (2003), *available at* http://www.socialworkers.org/ldf/legal_issue/200307.asp.

32. See §164.512(f), such disclosures may be made to a law enforcement officer if:

> required by law; in order to comply with a court or administrative order; to respond to an official request for purposes of identifying or locating a suspect, fugitive, or witness; to respond to an official request for information regarding a victim of a crime if the person agrees to disclose, or the entity cannot obtain consent due to incapacity or emergency circumstances; to alert law enforcement of the death of an individual that may have resulted from criminal conduct; the entity believes the information is evidence of a crime that occurred on its premises; the entity receives information while providing emergency health care "that appears necessary to alert law enforcement to ... " the commission of a crime, location of a crime, location of a victim, and location or identity of the perpetrator.

33. See §164.512(i) (only applicable after a waiver of individual authorization has been approved by an institutional review board or a privacy board).

34. *See* §164.512(j)(2) (information can not be disclosed if was learned through treatment for such criminal conduct or a request for such treatment).

35. See §164.512(k), such functions include:

> information authorities deem necessary for military missions or to determine eligibility of veteran benefits, information for purposes of national security and/or intelligence activities, information necessary to make medical suitability determinations, information correctional institutions and/or other custodial institutions deem necessary, and information shared between government programs that provide public benefits for purposes of determining eligibility and program administration.

36. §164.512(l).

37. *See* 45 C.F.R. §§ 160.202–203; *see also,* 45 C.F.R. §164.502; McKinney's CPLR §4508 (NY law only has 4 exceptions to confidentiality, unlike HIPAA).

38. NASW, *supra* note 22, *see also,* 45 C.F.R. §§ 160.202–203.

39. 551 P.2d 334 (Cal. 1976).

40. *Id.* at 340.

41. Under the common law, a person had no duty to protect a person from harm by a third party unless that person had some special relationship to either the dangerous person or the potential victim. These special relationships traditionally included parent–child, employer–employee, and driver–passenger. The unifying element of them is that there is some possibility of controlling the perpetrator and/or warning the victim about a foreseeable danger. In this century, the doctor–patient relationship was defined as "special," when the doctor knew of a patient's infectious disease. *Tarasoff* was the first reported case to extend "special" status to the psychotherapist–patient relationship.

42. 614 P.2d 728 (Cal. 1980).

43. Cal. Civ. Code §43.92.

44. *Ewing v. Goldstein,* 15 Cal. Rptr. 3d 864, 870 (Cal. Ct. App. 2004) (it is important to note that *Ewing* is an appellate court decision only binding in California's second district).

45. *Id.*

46. Cal. Evid. Code § 1010(c) (1996) (amended 1970).

47. *See, e.g.,* Arizona: *Little v. All Phoenix South Community Mental Health Center, Inc,* 186 Ariz. 97 (Ariz. App. 1995)(holding Ariz. Rev. Stat. Ann. § 36–517.02 requirement of a "clearly identifiable victim" to be unconstitutional); Indiana: Ind. Code 34–30–16–1; West Virginia: W.Va. Code Ann. § 27–3–1; Wisconsin: *Schuster v. Altenberg,* 144 Wis.2d 223 (Wis. 1988) (court recognized a duty to warn under Wisconsin tort law).

48. *See, e.g.,* California: Cal. Civ. Code § 43.92; Colorado: Colo. Rev. Stat. Ann. § 13–21–117 (1989); Delaware: Del. Code Ann. tit. 16 § 5402; Idaho: Idaho Code Ann. § 6–1902; Kentucky: Ky. Rev. Stat. Ann. §202A.400; Louisiana: La. Rev. St. § 9:2800.2 (1986); Maryland: Md. Code Ann., Cts. & Jud. Proc., § 5–609; Massachusetts: Mass. Gen. Laws. Ann. ch. 112 § 135A(c)(2) (1991) (amended 1993); Michigan: Mich. Comp. Laws Ann. § 330.1946; Minnesotaa: Minn. Stat. Ann. § 148.975; Mississippi: Miss. Code. Ann. §41–21–97 (1972) (amended 1991); Montana: Mont. Code Ann. § 27–1–1102; Nebraska: Neb. Rev. Stat. § 38–2137 (1993); New Hampshire: N.H. Rev. Stat. Ann. § 330-A:35; New Jersey: N.J. Stat. Ann. 2A:62A-16 (1991); Ohio: Ohio Rev. Code Ann. § 2305.51; Tennessee: Tenn. Code Ann. § 33–3–206; Utah: U.C.A. 1953 §78B-3–502; Vermont: *Peck v. Counseling Service of Addison County Inc.,* 146 Vt. 61 (Vt. 1985) (court recognized mental health professional's duty to warn); Virginia: Va. Code Ann. § 54.1–2400.1; Washington: Wash. Rev. Code Ann. § 71.05.120.

49. *E.g.,* Georgia, Kansas, Maine Nevada, North Carolina, North Dakota, and Pennsylvania: 50 Pa. Cons. Stat. Ann. § 7111.

50. *See, e.g.,* Alabama: *King v. Smith,* 539 So.2d 262 (Ala. 1989).

51. Iowa: Iowa Code Ann. § 154C.5.

52. Oklahoma: Okla. Stat. Ann. tit. 59, § 1261.6; Wyoming: Wyo. Stat. Ann. § 33–38–113.

53. 225 I.L.C.S. 20/16. Other states permitting but not requiring disclosure are: Alaska: Alaska Stat. § 08.95.900; Arkansas: Ark. Code Ann. § 17–103–107; Connecticut: Conn. Gen. Stat. Ann. § 52–146f; District of Columbia: D.C. Code § 7–1203.03; Florida: F.S.A. §491.0147; Hawaii: Haw. Rev. Stat. § 467E-15; Missouri: Mo. Ann. Stat: § 337.636; New Mexico: N.M. Stat. Ann. § 61–31–24; New York: N.Y. C.P.L.R. Law § 4508; Oregon: O.R.S. 40.252; Rhode Island: R.I. Gen. Laws § 5–37.3–4; South Carolina: S.C. Code Ann. § 19–11–95; Texas: Tex. Health & Safety Code Ann. § 611.004; South Dakota: S.D. Codified Laws § 27A-12–29.

54. *See, e.g.,* Wis. Stat. § 905.04(2) (permission to breach confidentiality when patient must be hospitalized because of mental illness) and *Schuster v. Altenberg,* 424 N.W. 2d 159 (Wis. 1988) (psychiatrist had duty to warn of patient's dangerous condition or seek commitment of her).

55. Mass. Gen. Laws. Ann. ch. 112 § 135A(c)(2) (1991).

56. *E.g., Boynton v. Burglass,* 590 So.2d 446 (Fla. Dist. Ct. App. 1991) (mental health practitioner lacks the requisite degree of control over patient to prevent patient from harming threatened third party).

57. *See supra* note 50.

58. Idaho Code § 54–3213.

59. *See* Carolyn Polowy, *Social Workers and Child Abuse Reporting,* Law Note Series (NASW 2000).

60. *See,* Child Abuse Prevention and Treatment and Adoption Reform, 42 U.S.C.A. § 5101 *et seq.* (1974) (amended 1988); 45 C.F.R. § 1340 (1979) (amended 1990).

61. *See, e.g., People v. Bowman,* 812 P.2d 725 (Colo. App. 1991); *N.H. v. District of Columbia,* 569 A.2d 1179 (App. D.C. 1990); *Young v. Arkansas Children's Hosp.,* 721 F. Supp. 197 (E.D. Ark. 1989); *Cozad v. Arkansas,* 792 S.W.2d 606 (Ark. 1990); *L.A.R. v. Ludwig,* 821 P.2d 291 (Ariz. App. 1991); *M. v. K.,* 452 A.2d 704 (N.J. Ch. 1982); *Matter of Jeanne T.T.,* 585 N.Y. S.2d 552 (App. Div. 1992); *People v. Tissois,* 526 N.E. 2d 1086 (N.Y. 1988).

62. *See, e.g.,* Cal. Penal Code §11172; *see also,* Carolyn Polowy, *Social Workers and Child Abuse Reporting,* Law Note Series (NASW 2000).

63. *See, e.g.,* Mass. Gen. Laws Ann. ch. 112 § 135A(g) (adults 60 years or older) and ch. 135A(h) (disabled adults); Ariz. Rev. Stat. § 46–454 (incapacitated or vulnerable adults).

64. *See* Carolyn Polowy, *Individual State Summaries of Mandated Reporting Requirements in Social Workers and Child Abuse Reporting,* Law Note Series (NASW 2000).

65. *See, e.g.,* Conn. Gen. Stat. § 52–146(c)(3); Mass. Gen. Law. ch. 112 § 135A(c)(1).

66. *See, e.g.,* Mass. Gen. Laws Ann. ch. 112 § 135A(c)(1).

67. *See, generally,* F. Reamer, Aids And Ethics (1993); Kenneth Labowitz, *Beyond Tarasoff: AIDS and the Obligation to Breach confidentiality,* 9 St. Louis U. Pub. L. Rev. 495 (1990); Paul Lombardo, *Legal Rights, Medical Remedies,* 1 Va. J. Soc. Pol'y & L. 475, 490 (1994).

68. *See, e.g., Chalk v. U.S. District Court,* 840 F.2d 701, 709–10 (9th Cir. 1988) (holding that teacher fired because of disclosure he had AIDS did not have to disprove every theoretical possibility of harm and that community's fear of disease did not justify denial of his right to continued employment).

69. *See* Lombardo, *supra* note 68, at 477–480.

70. *See, e.g.,* N.Y. Pub. Health. Law § 2782.4 (a)(3).

71. *See, e.g.,* N.Y. Pub. Health. Law § 2782.

72. *See, e.g.,* N.H. Rev. Stat. Ann. § 141-C:10

73. *See, e.g.,* N.Y. Pub. Health. Law § 2782.1(g).

74. *See, e.g.,* N.H. 1987 Op. Att'y Gen. 96. (Properly qualified members of the news media have a direct and tangible interest in vital statistic records when the information requested by them is of public nature.)

75. *See, e.g.,* N.Y. Pub. Health. Law § 2782.1(d).

76. 42 CFR 2.1 et. seq. (1994).

77. 42 CFR 2.31. (1994).

78. Substance Abuse and Mental Health Services Administration [hereafter, SAMHSA], *Frequently Asked Questions, available at* http://www.samhsa.gov/HealthPrivacy/docs/EHR-FAQs.pdf.

79. A bibliography listing articles, and cases on the subject of confidentiality and privilege is attached as Appendix C.

80. The spousal privilege prevents one member of a married couple from being compelled to testify against the other as to communications that took place in private between them. It dates back to the common law in the 16th century. *See Developments in the Law—Privileged Communications,* 98 Harv. L. Rev. 1629 (1985).

81. U.S. Const. amend. V.

82. *Jaffee v. Redmond,* 51 F.3d 1346, 1355–56 (7th Cir. 1995).

83. *In re Lifschutz,* 467 P.2d 557, 560 (Cal. 1970) (psychiatrist could not assert his own privacy interest in communications with former patient, where patient had waived his privilege under patient–litigant exception).

84. *See, e.g.,* La. Evid. Code, art. 510 B(2)(d).

85. *See, e.g., People v. Bass,* 529 N.Y.S.2d 961 (N.Y. Sup. Ct. 1988) (social worker correctly disclosed defendant's confidential communications of sexual abuse of minor child for purposes of child protection, but the incriminating statements could not be used against defendant in criminal prosecution).

86. *Caesar v. Mountanos,* 542 F.2d 1064 (Cal. App. 1976), *cert. denied,* 97 S.Ct. 1598.

87. *McMunn v. Florida,* 264 So.2d 868 (Fla. App. 1 Dist. 1972); *see also, State v. Pelley,* 828 N.E. 2d 915 (Ind. 2005) (privilege gives way during homicide proceedings when patient disclosure relates to the homicide or its immediate circumstances).

88. *Jaffee v. Redmond,* 116 S. Ct. 1923 (1996).

89. *Id.* at 1928 (citing *Trammel v. United States,* 445 U.S. 40 [1980]).

90. *Id.*

91. *Id.* at 1929.

92. *Id.*

93. *Id.* at 1931.

94. *Id.* at 1940.

95. *Id.* at 1931.

96. *Newton v. Kenna,* 354 F.3d 776 (8th Cir. 2004).

97. *Id.* at 785.

98. *Jaffee v. Redmond,* 518 U.S. 1, 18 n. 19 (1996).

99. *U.S. v. Glass,* 133 F.3d 1356 (10th Cir. 1998).

100. NASW, *Social Workers and Psychotherapist-Patient Privilege: Jaffee v. Redmond Revisited, available at* http://www.socialworkers.org/ldf/legal_issue/200503.asp.

101. *U.S. v. Glass,* 133 F.3d 1356, 1357 (10th Cir. 1998).

102. *U.S. v. Hayes,* 227 F.3d 578 (6th Cir. 2000).

103. *Id.* at 585.

104. *United States v. Chase,* 340 F.3d 978 (9th Cir. 2003).

105. *U.S. v. Auster,* 517 F.3d 312 (5th Cir. 2008).

106. *Id.* at 315.

107. *Auster v. U.S.,* 129 S.Ct. 312 (2008).

108. NASW, *supra* note 108.

109. Ninety-two state cases have positively cited and/or discussed the *Jaffee* ruling.

(g) Social workers should inform clients involved in family, couples, marital, or group counseling of the social worker's, employer's, and/or agency's policy concerning the social worker's disclosure of confidential information among the parties involved in the counseling.

(h) Social workers should not disclose confidential information to third party payors, unless client's have authorized such disclosure.

(i) Social workers should not discuss confidential information in any setting unless privacy can be assured. Social workers should not discuss confidential information in public or semi-public areas (such as hallways, waiting rooms, elevators, and restaurants).

(j) Social workers should protect the confidentiality of clients during legal proceedings to the extent permitted by law. When a court of law or other legally authorized body orders social workers to disclose confidential or privileged information without a client's consent and such disclosure could cause harm to the client, social workers should request that the court withdraw or limit the order as narrowly as possible and/or maintain the records under seal, unavailable for public inspection.

(k) Social workers should protect the confidentiality of clients when responding to requests from members of the media.

(l) Social workers should protect the confidentiality of clients' written and electronic records and other sensitive information. Social workers should take reasonable steps to ensure that clients' records are stored in a secure location and that clients' records are not available to others who are not authorized to have access.

(m) Social workers should take precautions to ensure and maintain the confidentiality of information transmitted to other parties through the use of computers, electronic mail, facsimile machines, telephones and telephone answering machines, and other electronic or computer technology. Disclosure of identifying information should be avoided whenever possible.

(n) Social workers should transfer or dispose of clients' records in a manner that protects clients' confidentiality and is consistent with state statutes governing records and social work licensure.

(o) Social workers should take reasonable precautions to protect client confidentiality in the event of the social worker's termination of practice, incapacitation, or death.

(p) Social workers should not disclose identifying information when discussing clients for teaching or training purposes, unless the client has consented to disclosure of confidential information.

(q) Social workers should not disclose identifying information when discussing clients with consultants, unless the client has consented to disclosure of confidential information or there is a compelling need for such disclosure.

(r) Social workers should protect the confidentiality of deceased clients consistent with the preceding standards.

Note: See *supra* note 1, at §1.07.

Appendix B

Review of SAMHSA's *Frequently Asked Questions: Applying The Substance Abuse Confidentiality Regulations To Health Information Exchange*

- Federal law does allow substance abuse treatment programs to include information on patients' substance use disorders in electronic health information exchange systems. However the regulations require the patient's consent,[a] with a few exceptions.[b]

- When the patient is a minor, consent must be received from the minor, and depending on state law, also the minor's parent or guardian.[c]

- When patient information is disclosed, the substance abuse treatment program must ensure that "each disclosure made with written patient consent [is] ... accompanied by a written statement that the information disclosed is protected by federal law and that the recipient cannot make any further disclosure of it unless permitted by the regulations."[d]

- A third party entity holding electronic patient information (an HIO), based on an agreement to provide services to a substance abuse treatment program, may disclose the patient information to its own contract agents without the patients' consent,[e] in order to provide the services in the agreement with the substance abuse treatment program. The contract agent may only disclose the information it receives to the HIO or to the substance abuse program where the information originated.

- An HIO may disclose patients' demographic information without the patients' consent., as long as it "does not reveal any information that would identify the person, either directly or indirectly, as having a current or past drug or alcohol problem or as being a patient in a Part 2 program."[f]

- If information is released without consent due to a medical emergency, the information can be re-disclosed without the patient's consent. However "it must be limited to information necessary to carry out the purpose of the disclosure (42 CFR § 2.13[a])."[g]

- Please refer to SAMHSA's *Frequently Asked Questions* for further detailed information on the confidentiality regulations and health information exchange.

Notes

a. Patient's consent must be in writing and contain specific elements, see SAMHSA, *supra* note 79, at 8–9.

b. Unlike HIPAA, the exceptions do not include disclosure for purposes of treatment, payment, or health care operations. They do include physical and mental health medical emergencies (the existence of which can be determined by any health care provider treating the patient for the medical emergency), audits, and evaluations. See 42 CFR §§ 2.3, 2.12, 2.13, 2.5.

c. In other words, if a state law gives a minor the legal authority to consent to treatment on his/her own, without a parent's or guardian's permission or knowledge, then only the minor's consent is required for the HIO to disclose the minor's information to the HIO affiliated health care provider under Part 2. If state law requires parental consent for the minor to be provided alcohol or drug treatment, then the consent of both the minor patient and the parent or guardian is required before the Part 2 program or HIO can make any disclosures. The minor's written consent must be obtained first in all cases. SAMHSA, *supra* note 79, at 17.

d. SAMHSA, *supra* note 79, at 9.

e. This may be done to provide the services in the agreement with the substance abuse treatment program. The contract agent may only disclose the information it receives to the HIO or to the substance abuse program where the information originated.

f. The information must "not reveal any information that would identify the person, either directly or indirectly, as having a current or past drug or alcohol problem or as being a patient in a Part 2 program." SAMHSA, *supra* note 79, at 10.

g. The information " must be limited to information necessary to carry out the purpose of the disclosure (42 CFR § 2.13[a])."SAMHSA, *supra* note 79, at 16.

Appendix C

Social Worker–Client Privilege and Confidentiality Laws

States have varying laws regarding confidentiality and privilege. The chart below lists applicable statutes and regulations for each state. All states address the confidentiality requirements for social workers through statute or regulation. Some states do not have separate confidentiality provisions but address the issue in the same statutes as privilege. As the chart demonstrates, some states have a generic privilege statute that social workers may invoke whereas others have specific privilege statutes applicable only to social workers. A small minority of states do not allow social workers to invoke the privilege at all.

APPENDIX A: Social Worker–Client Privilege and Confidentiality Laws

STATE	GENERIC PRIVILEGE STATUTE FOR ALL MENTAL HEALTH PROFESSIONALS	SPECIFIC PRIVILEGE STATUTE FOR SOCIAL WORKERS	STATUTE OR CASE SPECIFICALLY EXCLUDING SOCIAL WORKERS	CONFIDENTIALITY STATUTE
Alabama				Ala. Admin. Code r.850-x-9-.01
Alaska			Alaska Stat. § 08.95.900(a)(4); ***Alfred v. Alaska,*** 554 P.2d 411 (1976)	AS § 08.95.900
Arizona	Ariz. Rev.Stat. §32–3283			Ariz. Admin. Code R4–6–1105
Arkansas		Ark. Code Ann. § 17–103–107		Ark. Admin. Code 120.00.1-X
California	Cal. Evid. Code § 1014			Cal. Bus. & Prof. Code §4992.3(n), Cal Admin. Code tit. 16 §1881(i)
Colorado	Colo. Rev. Stat. §13–90–107(1)(g)			Colo. Rev. Stat. § 12–43–218
Connecticut		Conn. Gen. Stat. Ann. §52–146q		***See*** Conn. Gen. Stat. Ann. §52–146q(b)
Delaware		D.R.E. Rule 503		24 Del. Code § 3913
District of Columbia	D.C. Code § 14–307			DC ST 7–1201.02

STATE	GENERIC PRIVILEGE STATUTE FOR ALL MENTAL HEALTH PROFESSIONALS	SPECIFIC PRIVILEGE STATUTE FOR SOCIAL WORKERS	STATUTE OR CASE SPECIFICALLY EXCLUDING SOCIAL WORKERS	CONFIDENTIALITY STATUTE
Florida	Fla. Stat. Ann. § 90.503			F.S.A. §491.0147
Georgia	Ga.Code Ann. § 24–9–21			Ga. Comp. R. & Regs. 135–7-.03
Hawaii		Haw. Rev. Stat. § 467E-15		HRS §626–1
Idaho		Idaho Code § 54–3213		ID ADC 24.14.01.450
Illinois		225 I.L.C.S. § 20/16		68 Ill. Adm. Code 1470.96
Indiana		Ind. Code Ann. § 25–23.6–6–1		***See*** Ind. Code Ann. § 25–23.6–6–1
Iowa	Iowa Code Ann. § 622.10			Iowa Code Ann. §154C.5
Kansas		Kan. Stat. Ann. § 65–6315		***See*** Kan. Stat. Ann. § 65–6315
Kentucky	Ky. R. Evid., Rule 507			201 Ky Admin. Regs. 23:080
Louisiana	La. Evid. Code art. 510			La. Admin. Code tit. 46, pt. XXV, §115
Maine		32 Me. Rev. Stat. Ann. § 7005		***See*** 32 Me. Rev. Stat. Ann. § 7005
Maryland		Md. Code, Cts. & Jud. Proc. § 9–121		MD ADC 10.42.02.03
Massachusetts		M.G.L.A. §135B		M.G.L.A. 112 §135A
Michigan		M.C.L.A. 333.18513		***See*** M.C.L.A. 333.18513
Minnesota	Minn. Stat. Ann. § 595.02 (g)			Minn. R. 8740.0330
Mississippi		Miss. Code. Ann. § 73–53–29		Miss. Admin. Code 30–14–1:A-VII(B) (20)
Missouri	Mo. Rev. Stats. § 337.636			20 Mo. Code of State Regulations 2263–3.100
Montana		Mont. Code Ann. §37–22–401		Mont. Admin. R. 24.219.801
Nebraska	Neb. Rev. Stat. § 38–2136			172 NAC Ch. 94, s. 016–018

STATE	GENERIC PRIVILEGE STATUTE FOR ALL MENTAL HEALTH PROFESSIONALS	SPECIFIC PRIVILEGE STATUTE FOR SOCIAL WORKERS	STATUTE OR CASE SPECIFICALLY EXCLUDING SOCIAL WORKERS	CONFIDENTIALITY STATUTE
Nevada		Nev. Rev. Stat. §§ 49.251–49.252		NAC 641B.210
New Hampshire	N.H.Rev.Stat.Ann. § 330-A:32			N.H. Code Admin. R. Mhp 501.02
New Jersey		N.J. Stat. Ann. § 45:15BB-13		N.J.A.C. 13:44G-12.3
New Mexico		N.M. Stat. Ann. § 61–31–24		N.M. Admin. Code 16.63.16
New York		N.Y. Civ. Prac. L&R. § 4508		***See*** N.Y. Civ. Prac. L&R. § 4508
North Carolina		N.C. Gen. Stat. § 8–53.7		21 N.C.A.C. 63.0507
North Dakota			***N.D. v. Copeland,*** 448 N.W.2d 611 (1989) , ***State v. Clark,*** 570 N.W. 2d 195 (N.D. 1997)	N.D. Admin Code §75.5–02–06.1–01
Ohio	Ohio Rev. Code Ann. § 2317.02(G)			Ohio Admin Code §4757–5–01
Oklahoma		59 Okl. St. Ann. § 1261.6		Okla. Admin. Code 675:20–1–6
Oregon		Or. Rev. Stat. § 40.250		Or. Admin. R. 877–030–0070
Pennsylvania				49 Pa. Code §47.72
Rhode Island		R.I. Gen. Laws § 5–39.1–4		R.I. Admin Code 31–5–27:7.0
South Carolina	S.C. Code § 19–11–95			S.C. Code of Regulations R.110–20
South Dakota		S.D. Codified Laws § 36–26–30		***See*** S.D. Codified Laws § 36–26–30
Tennessee		Tenn. Code. Ann. §63–23–109		TN ADC 1365–01-.10
Texas	Tex. R. Civ. Evid., Rule 510			22 TAC §781.411
Utah	Utah Rules of Evidence, Rule 506			Utah Code Ann. § 58–60–114

STATE	GENERIC PRIVILEGE STATUTE FOR ALL MENTAL HEALTH PROFESSIONALS	SPECIFIC PRIVILEGE STATUTE FOR SOCIAL WORKERS	STATUTE OR CASE SPECIFICALLY EXCLUDING SOCIAL WORKERS	CONFIDENTIALITY STATUTE
Vermont	Vermont Rule of Evidence, Rule 503			***See*** Vermont Rule of Evidence, Rule 503(a)(6)
Virginia	Va. Code § 8.01–400.2			18VAC140–20–150
Washington	Wash. Rev. Code. Ann. §5.60.060(9)			Wash. Rev. Code. Ann. § 18.19.180
West Virginia		W. Va. Code § 30–30–12		W. VA. C.S.R. §25–1–4
Wisconsin	Wis. Stat. Ann. § 905.04			Wis. Adm. Code s MPSW 20.02
Wyoming		Wyo. Stat. Ann. § 33–38–113		WY Rules and Regulations AI MH Ch. 11 s. 2

Appendix D

Bibliography

Law Journal Articles

Catherine Baytion, *Toward Uniform Application of a Federal Psychotherapist-Patient Privilege,* 70 Wash. L. Rev. 153 (1995).

Fillmore Buckner, *"Where the Public Peril Begins": 25 Years After Tarasoff,* 21 J. Legal Med. 187 (2000).

W. Jonathan Cardi, *A Pluralistic Analysis of the Therapist/Physician Duty to Warn Third Parties,* 44 Wake Forest L. Rev. 877 (2009).

Phyllis Coleman, *Warning a Patient's Intended Victim While Preserving Testimonial Privilege,* 77-Aug Fla. B. J. 20 (2003).

Evidence—Sixth Circuit Holds That Tarasoff Disclosures Do Not Vitiate Psychotherapist-Patient Privilege, Untied States v. Hayes, 227 F.3d 578 (6Th Cir. 2000), 114 Harv. L. Rev. 2194 (2001).

Brian Ginsberg, *Therapists Behaving Badly: Why the Tarasoff Duty is not Always Economically Efficient,* 43 Willamette L. Rev. 31 (2007).

Brian Ginsberg, *Tarasoff at Thirty: Victim's Knowledge Shrinks the Psychotherapist's Duty to Warn and Protect,* 21 J. Contemp. Health L. & Pol'y 1 (2004).

Margaret Hopson, *Bitter Medicine: A Critical Look at the Mental Health Care Provider's Duty to Warn in Texas,* 31 St. Mary's L. J. 359 (2000).

Michelle King, *Physician Duty to Warn a Patient's Offspring of Hereditary Genetic Defects: Balancing The Patient's Right to Confidentiality Against the Family Member's Right to Know- Can or Should Tarasoff Apply,* 4 Quinnipiac Health L. J. 1 (2000).

Elisia Klinka, *It's Been a Privilege: Advising Patients of the Tarasoff Duty and its Legal Consequences for the Federal Psychotherapist-Patient Privilege,* 78 Fordham L. Rev. 863 (2009).

Heidi Lewis, *Third Parties Beware: The Texas Supreme Court Strengthens Psychotherapist-Client Confidentiality in Thapar v. Zezulka,* 1 Hous. J. Health L. & Pol'y 263 (2001).

Theo Liebmann, *Confidentiality, Consultation, and the Child Client,* 75 Temp. L. Rev. 821, 862 (2002).

Brian McKeever, *Contours and Chaos: A Proposal for Courts to Apply the "Dangerous Patient" Exception to the Psychotherapist Patient Privilege*, 34 N.M. L. Rev. 109 (2004).

Gretchen Obrist, *The Nebraska Supreme Court Lets Its Probation Department Off the Hook in Bartunek v. State, 266 Neb. 454, 666 N.W.2D 435 (2003): "No Duty" as a Non Response to Violence to Against Women and Identifiable Victims*, 83 Neb. L. Rev. 225, 294 (2004).

Deborah Paruch, *The Psychotherapist Patient Privilege in the Family Court: An Exemplar of Disharmony Between Social Policy Goals, Professional Ethics, and the Current State of the Law*, 29 N. Ill. U. L. Rev. 499 (2009).

Elizabeth Roberson-Young, *Untangling Charlotte's Web: Balancing the Confidentiality Rights of Patients and Third-Party Negligent-Therapy Claims in Johnson v. Rogers Memorial Hospital*, 2006 Wis. L. Rev. 1683 (2006).

Scott Rogge, *Liability for Psychiatrists under New York Law for Failing to Identify Dangerous Patients*, 20 Pace L. Rev. 221 (2000).

Paul Salamanca, *Constitutional Protection for Conversations Between Therapists and Clients*, 64 Mo. L. Rev. 77, (1999).

Christopher Slobogin, *Tarasoff as a Duty to Treat: Insights from Criminal Law*, 75 U. Cin. L. Rev. 645 (2006).

Cases

Bohrn v. Klick, 276 S.W.3d 863 (Mo. Ct. App. 2009) (social worker-client privilege found to be inapplicable in proceedings regarding child abuse, neglect, or welfare of children).

Commonwealth v. Pelosi, 55 Mass. App. Ct. 390 (Mass. App. Ct. 2002) (social worker's report on suspected child abuse did not constitute as waiver of social worker privilege regarding child's counseling records).

Ewing v. Northridge Hospital Medical Center, 16 Cal Rptr. 3d 591, 598 (Cal. Ct. App. 2004) (psychotherapist's duty to warn still applies when threat patient poses is communicated to the psychotherapist by patient's relative to facilitate treatment, rather than the patient himself).

In re Kristina W., 94 Cal. App. 4th 521 (Cal. Ct. App. 2001) (psychotherapist-patient privilege does not preclude therapist from disclosing information against minor's wishes to accomplish "the information-gathering role of therapy" in child dependency proceedings).

In re S.A., 182 Cal. App. 4th 1128 (Cal. Ct. App. 2010) (disclosures to the police regarding abuse did not waive the psychotherapist-patient privilege, as client is the holder of the privilege and did not authorize such disclosures).

In the Matter of L.F., 995 A.2d 356 (Pa. Super. Ct. 2010) (patient-therapist privilege abrogated in parental termination proceedings where social worker compelled to provide limited testimony regarding client's compliance with and progress in sex abuse therapy).

Jaffee v. Redmond, 116 S. Ct. 1923 (1996); available at http://scholar.google.com/scholar_case?case=3659760322684331 31&hl=en&as_sdt=2&as_vis=1&oi=scholarr.

Jane Doe v. Maryland Board of Social Work Examiners, 384 Md. 161 (Md. 2004) (social worker-client privilege yields to Board of Social Work Examiner's subpoena for client records when investigating allegations that social worker breached professional duties by not reporting client's suspected child abuse).

Kasdaglis v. Department of Health of the State of Florida, 827 So. 2d 328 (Fla. Dist. Ct. App. 2002) (social worker cannot be disciplined for informing parent of minor-patient that patient may hurt himself, under the physical harm exception to psychologist-patient privilege).

Lichtenberg v. Office of Professional Regulation, 987 A.2d 322 (Vt. 2009) (social worker did not violate NASW Code of Ethics regarding conflicts of interest by providing family therapy to father and child, and providing recommendations to guardian ad litem concerning father's interactions with child in custody dispute).

Magnus v. Department of Professional Regulation, 359 Ill. App.3d 773 (Ill. App. Ct. 2005) (duty to report child abuse applies where the client is a minor teenager having a consensual sexual relationship with another teenager, and abrogates the social worker-client privilege) (social worker's failure to comply with statutory duty to report abuse may constitute malpractice and result in license suspension).

Newton v. Kenna, 354 F.3d 776 (8th Cir. 2004) (psychotherapist-patient privilege barred defendant's motion to review prosecution witness's psychiatric records for purposes of cross examination).

People v. Sergio, 21 Misc. 3d 451 (N.Y. Sup. Ct. 2008) (social worker may testify about confidential information where child under 16 is victim of abuse, but only where child not the parent is the client of the social worker).

Pinnell v. State, 838 So. 2d 596 (Fla. Dist. Ct. App. 2003) (social worker-client communications protected under sexual assault counselor-victim privilege).

S.C. v. Guardian Ad Litem, 845 So. 2d. 953 (Fla. Dist. Ct. App. 2003) (minor can assert psychotherapist-patient privilege to deny guardian ad-litem's access to therapeutic records).

State v. Herendeen, 279 Ga. 323 (Ga. 2005) (mental health provider-patient privilege used to quash subpoena for victim/patient's records in child molestation case, even though therapy was court mandated).

State v. Orr, 291 Conn. 642 (Conn. 2009) (dangerous client exception to social worker-client confidentiality does not permit social worker's testimony in client's criminal trial).

State v. Orwick, 153 Ohio App. 3d. 88 (Ohio Ct. App. 2003) (social worker did not have standing to assert defendant's privilege when court ordered disclosure of communications between social worker and defendant) (some statements being excepted from the privilege does not mean client's full records to be disclosed).

State v. Spencer, 198 Or. App. 599 (Or. Ct. App. 2005) (in child abuse proceeding psychotherapist-patient privilege is abrogated regardless of whether patient is perpetrator of abuse or the victim, found irrelevant that Oregon statute exempts psychotherapists from the obligation to report suspected child abuse).

State v. Pelley, 828 N.E. 2d 915 (Ind. 2005) (social workers considered counselors for purposes of counselor-patient privilege, and privilege gives way during homicide proceedings when patient disclosure relates to the homicide or its immediate circumstances).

Tarasoff v. Regents of Univ. of Cal., 551 P.2d 334 (Cal. 1976) (California recognized duty of psychotherapist to protect third parties from the foreseeable harm of a client).

Thompson v. Chapman, 176 Ohio App.3d 334 (Ohio Ct. App. 2008) (case by case in camera review needed to determine if psychiatric records are 'medical' records, which can be disclosed if related to injuries relevant to issues of case, or 'counseling' records, that can only be disclosed if statutory exception exists).

U.S. v. Auster, 517 F.3d 312 (5th Cir. 2008) (defendant was aware of therapist's statutory duty to report threats, therefore threats he made during therapy were admissible against him in his trial).

U.S. v. Glass, 133 F.3d 1356 (10th Cir. 1998) (based on *Jaffee*, found existence of 'dangerous patient' exception to psychotherapist-patient privilege).

U.S. v. Hayes, 227 F.3d 578 (6th Cir. 2000) (there is no 'dangerous patient' exception to the psychotherapist-patient privilege in criminal proceedings).

U.S. v. Chase, 340 F.3d 978 (9th Cir. 2003) (refused to recognize a 'dangerous patient' exception to the psychotherapist-patient privilege in criminal proceedings).

NASW Resources

F. Reamer, ETHICAL STANDARDS IN SOCIAL WORK, A REVIEW OF THE NASW CODE OF ETHICS (2006).

National Association of Social Workers [hereafter, NASW], HIPAA AMENDMENTS FOR A NEW DECADE: 2010 AND BEYOND, available at http://www.socialworkers.org/ldf/legal_issue/2010/201002.asp.

NASW, LEGAL ISSUES: RECENT DEVELOPMENTS IN CONFIDENTIALITY AND PRIVILEGE, IN ENCYCLOPEDIA OF SOCIAL WORK (20th Edition, 2008).

NASW, NASW STANDARDS FOR CLINICAL SOCIAL WORK IN SOCIAL WORK PRACTICE (2005).

NASW, PSYCHOTHERAPIST-PATIENT PRIVILEGE IN THE MILITARY (2005), available at http://www.socialworkers.org/ldf/legal_issue/200507.asp; see Uniform Code of Military, Justice, MRE 513.

NASW, SCHOOL SOCIAL WORKERS AND CONFIDENTIALITY (2008), available at http://www.socialworkers.org/ldf/legal_issue/2008/200804.asp.

NASW, SOCIAL WORKERS AND DUTY TO WARN STATE LAWS (2008), available at http://www.socialworkers.org/ldf/legal_issue/2008/200802.asp.